THE WORLD OF MARTIAL ARTS
NINJA

BY JIM OLLHOFF

Visit us at
www.abdopublishing.com

Published by ABDO Publishing Company, 8000 West 78th Street, Suite 310, Edina, MN 55439.
Copyright ©2008 by Abdo Consulting Group, Inc. International copyrights reserved in all countries.
No part of this book may be reproduced in any form without written permission from the publisher.
ABDO & Daughters™ is a trademark and logo of ABDO Publishing Company.

Printed in the United States.

Editor: John Hamilton
Graphic Design: John Hamilton
Cover Design: Neil Klinepier
Cover Illustration: iStockphoto
Interior Photos and Illustrations: p 1 boy dressed as ninja, iStockphoto; p 5 ninja behind tree, courtesy
Ninja Store; p 6 group of samurai, Corbis; p 7 map of Japan, Getty Images; p 7 (inset) globe view of
Japan, iStockphoto; p 8 samurai riding horse, Corbis; p 9 Matsumoto Castle, iStockphoto; p 10 ninja
with sword, iStockphoto; p 13 ninja reenactor with sword, Getty Images; p 15 ninjas scaling castle wall,
courtesy Ninja Store; p 16 group of ninjas, iStockphoto; p 17 ninja in water with sword, iStockphoto;
p 19 boy dressed as ninja, iStockphoto; p 20 woman wearing red ninja uniform, Getty Images; p 21 man
wearing black ninja uniform, Getty Images; p 22 (top) man holding ninja sword, iStockphoto;
p 22 (middle) kusarigama, John Hamilton; p 22 (bottom) shuriken, John Hamilton; p 24 "flying" ninja,
Getty Images; p 25 crouching ninja unsheathing sword, Corbis; p 26 three ninja on hill, iStockphoto;
p 28 Masaaki Hatsumi with student, AP Images; p 29 Masaaki Hatsumi teaching class, AP Images;
p 31 samurai sword, iStockphoto.

Library of Congress Cataloging-in-Publication Data

Ollhoff, Jim, 1959-
   Ninja / Jim Ollhoff.
      p. cm. -- (World of martial arts)
   Includes index.
   ISBN 978-1-59928-982-3
   1. Ninja. 2. Ninjutsu. I. Title.
   UB271.J3O44 2008
   355.3'432--dc22
                         2007030552

CONTENTS

Who Were the Ninjas?.. 4

History of the Ninjas.. 6

Japan's Secret Weapons.. 12

Ninja Tactics... 14

Ninja Training.. 18

Clothing and Weapons.. 20

Ninja Myths... 24

Are There Ninjas Today?... 28

Glossary.. 30

Index... 32

WHO WERE THE NINJAS?

Japan, 1550 A.D.: Several samurai bodyguards keep watch in the house of their clan leader. At midnight, they hear a faint, muffled groan. They quickly open the sliding door to the room of their clan leader. They find him lying on the floor, dead. A mysterious figure, clothed in black, crouches next to the body. The bodyguards charge into the room, swords drawn. Suddenly, a blinding flash knocks them to the ground. When they open their eyes, the mysterious figure is gone. The clan leader is dead, a victim of a poison dart to his neck. There were no signs of a forced entry. All the doors were locked from the inside. No one could possibly have gotten in or out, yet the clan leader was murdered. It was the work of a ninja.

Ninjas, sometimes called *shinobi* in the Japanese language, practiced a martial art called ninjitsu. From about 1400 to 1600 A.D., ninjas were important to the armies of Japan. The job of the ninja was to spy on the enemy, assassinate enemy leaders, and cause general confusion. They did everything in secret. They snuck into an enemy's castle, completed their mission, and then snuck back out. They were soldiers-for-hire, highly skilled warriors who would sell their services to the highest bidder.

Stories about ninjas were often told in medieval Japan. These stories were amazing, and people began to believe everything they heard about ninjas. However, the stories were rarely true. But the myths created an atmosphere of fear and mystery. Today, because of their starring roles in movies and cartoons, ninjas are more popular than ever.

Above: A lone ninja hides behind a tree, sword in hand. A shuriken is stuck to the tree trunk.

HISTORY OF THE NINJAS

Below: Samurai warriors were professional soldiers who fought for warlords in medieval Japan.

Japan is an island nation on the west side of the Pacific Ocean, near the Asian mainland. For most of its history, it did not have a single government or a single ruler. Through much of its history, there was constant fighting between clans struggling for power. A warlord would gather together men from the area, give them swords, and try to expand his territory. The neighboring clan leader would need to defend his land, and perhaps engage in a counterattack.

When clan leaders needed armies, they had to recruit the soldiers. They went to a village, found farmers and merchants, and gave them swords. The leaders pushed the untrained men into battle, with no armor. They weren't professional soldiers or military men.

It soon became apparent to the warlords and clan leaders that a few professionally trained warriors were more effective than a lot of farmers with swords. So, there arose a class of soldiers called the *samurai*. The samurai were brave and strong warriors who trained constantly in weapons and martial arts. They were legendary for their skill on the battlefield. Warlords and clan leaders employed the samurai, who swore oaths of loyalty to their leaders.

Left: A map of modern-day Japan.

Above: A samurai warrior rides into battle.

The samurai were not only famous for their battlefield skills. They were also famous for their code of honor. They committed themselves to defending their leader, maintaining honor, and never doing anything deceitful or dishonest. Of course, many samurai didn't live up to the code, but most samurai took their oath very seriously. They held so tightly to their code of honor that if they did anything to dishonor themselves or their leader, they would commit *seppuku*—they would take their own life.

The warlords and clan leaders liked having samurai, of course. However, it also presented them with a problem. The samurai would refuse to sneak into a castle to assassinate anyone, because that would be dishonorable. Sabotaging the enemy's food supply, creating confusion in the enemy camp, or sneaking around to gather information about enemy plans—those would all be dishonorable acts. The samurai simply refused to do them.

However, the warlords needed information about enemy plans, and they sometimes wanted to assassinate enemy generals. So, the warlords hired ninjas. The ninjas were skilled in assassinations, gathering intelligence, and creating confusion among the enemy. A single ninja could sneak into an enemy castle at night, climb up into the rafters, and listen to the enemy generals talk about their strategy. The ninja could then sneak away from the castle and deliver the crucial information to his employer.

Above: Japan's Matsumoto Castle. Ninjas were highly skilled at sneaking into seemingly invincible places like this fortress.

Samurai hated the ninjas because they did dishonorable things. Ninjas were mercenaries—people who fought only if they were well paid. However, the warlords needed them, and used them. The ninja were in an unusual position— they were hated and feared, but important and needed. So, if the samurai wouldn't do something—maybe the ninjas would.

Japanese authors began writing about ninjas in the 1400s, although people spied on enemies and engaged in other ninja-like activities long before that. In the mid 1400s, a few samurai families began to practice ninjitsu. They practiced in secret, passing on their tactics to only a few students or family members.

The worst of the clan fighting happened from about 1450 A.D. to about 1600 A.D. During this time, the use of ninjas was at its peak. After 1600, one of the warlords emerged as the victor. His name was Tokugawa Ieyasu, and he became the *shogun*, the leader of the entire country. He unified Japan, bringing an end to the civil wars and clan battles. After this, the need for ninjas declined, and many ninjas took jobs as palace guards. The last recorded account of the use of a ninja in battle is from the year 1638.

Facing page: Ninjas fought only if they were well paid. Japanese warlords were often forced to buy the ninjas' services, which included intelligence gathering and assassination—things most samurai warriors believed were dishonorable and refused to do.

Japan's Secret Weapons

The two most important ninja clans developed in the Japanese provinces of Iga and Koga. These two areas were near each other in a region that was difficult to get to because of the mountains on all sides. Yet, Iga and Koga provinces were in the middle of the Japanese main island of Honshu. Warring clans often passed through the area on their way to battle. The ninjas sold their services to whoever paid the most. Warfare was very common in medieval Japan, which was good for the ninja business.

The samurai swore an oath of allegiance to their masters. Ninjas did not. They were mercenaries, working for whoever would pay them. Sometimes a ninja would work for one person, and then a few years later work for the enemy of the first employer.

One of the early stories tells about a ninja, Nakagawa Shoshunjin, who was trying to persuade a general named Gemban to hire him. General Gemban jokingly said, "I'll hire you only if you can steal my pillow as I sleep." That night, the sound of a rainstorm awakened General Gemban. The general lay on his bed, with his head on his pillow. Then he felt a drop of water on his forehead. And then another. He sighed, "Another leak in the roof."

General Gemban raised his head briefly to reposition himself on the bed so the raindrops wouldn't hit him anymore. When he put his head back down, to his surprise, his pillow was gone. He sat up quickly. Next to the bed was Nakagawa Shoshunjin. The ninja was smiling and holding the general's pillow. The general hired him immediately. Whether or not the story is true, it tells how important the ninjas' skills were to the military of the time.

Above: A ninja reenactor at a castle in Japan.

Ninja Tactics

Ninjas were the secret agents of medieval Japan. They routinely performed three tasks: spying on the enemy, assassinating enemy leaders, and working to cause confusion or hinder the enemy's war effort.

Ninjas had many ways to sneak into castles. The most common way was simply to disguise themselves. They might pretend to be monks or merchants. Sometimes they dressed like castle residents so they could come and go as they pleased. Large family groups sometimes carried lanterns with the family emblem on it. Ninjas often stole such lanterns and marched into the castle, pretending to be with the larger group.

Another way to sneak into a castle was to climb up and over the outer wall. If the wall was unattended, ninjas could often scale it using special climbing equipment. They relied on the darkness of night to slip into the castle without being noticed.

Sometimes, however, castle guards maintained lamps along the top of the wall. This was so they could keep watch at night. One technique the ninjas used was to fire a primitive rifle (called an arquebus) at the guards on the wall. The guards would then immediately put out the lamps so that the attackers with the guns couldn't see them. However, this was exactly what the ninjas wanted them to do. Since the wall was now dark, the ninjas could scale it under the cover of darkness.

Above: Ninjas often sneaked into castles by disguising themselves as monks or merchants. When that didn't work, they sometimes climbed up castle walls, usually at night.

When the ninjas got into a castle, they could do a lot of mischief. They might destroy or poison the food supply. They might hide in the rafters of a building and listen to the enemy generals as they made plans. Sometimes they assassinated enemy leaders.

One of the ninjas' favorite methods of causing confusion was to sneak into a castle and start fires. If they could slip in and out without being noticed, those in the castle would start to be suspicious of each other, believing someone was a traitor. The ninjas, in whatever task they were given, were an important part of a warlord's total plan.

Below: Ninjas caused confusion by attacking in groups and creating distractions.

Some warlords became so fearful of ninjas that they began to develop special anti-ninja tactics. One such invention was called a nightingale floor. This was a series of hinges and squeaky floorboards, so that when a person put weight on the floor it would let out a loud creak. No one could walk across the floor without making a lot of noise. Guards immediately knew if someone was approaching. Other anti-ninja tactics included trap doors and hidden escape routes.

One of the most famous ninja assassinations is a gruesome story, and historians still debate whether it is true or not. It is said that a ninja sneaked into the home of the leader Uesugi Kenshin. According to the legend, the ninja entered the outhouse, quietly submerging himself in the sewage pit under the toilet, where he waited patiently. According to the story, when Kenshin finally went to use the toilet, he was killed by a spear from below.

Below: A ninja lurks under the water.

Ninja Training

Ninja children, like samurai children, were born into their profession. Fathers trained their children from an early age—as soon as they learned to walk. Children born into a samurai clan learned martial arts, the art of the sword, as well as poetry and philosophy. Children born into ninja clans learned martial arts, the use of poisons and explosives, and the art of stealth.

There were different forms, or schools, of ninjitsu. The school known as Togakure Ryu ninjitsu emphasized 18 levels of training. The first level is knowledge of self. The ninjas had to know their own strengths and weaknesses. Ninjas couldn't afford the delusion that they were good at everything. Their lives might depend on knowledge of what they could do, and what they could not do.

The second level of training is unarmed combat, which is called *tai jutsu*. It is more free flowing than most martial arts. It attempts to use a person's natural body motions. Instead of learning new blocks, new punches and kicks, or new joint locks, tai jutsu stylists learn to defend and attack in natural ways, following the body's natural motions.

The next five levels of training are with weapons—the bo, spear, and many others. After that, ninjas learned about explosives. They also learned how to disguise themselves. After all, a good disguise is more than just putting on a costume—ninjas were sometimes like actors who had to play a part.

Left: Ninja training began at a very young age, sometimes as early as two or three years old.

The eleventh level of training is called shinobi-iri, which is the art of stealth. This art teaches how to walk quietly, how to climb, and how to break into buildings without being noticed. The next level is horsemanship—ninjas were expected to be expert riders. Water training is the next level, which included swimming, floating undetected, and even underwater fighting techniques.

After that, the ninjas learned strategy, spying, and escape. Finally, they learned about the weather and geography, since those elements could be very important in a battle.

CLOTHING AND WEAPONS

Facing page: A basic black ninja uniform.
Below: Red uniforms hid bloodstains. Female ninjas were called kunoichi.

Ninjas are frequently pictured wearing all-black uniforms, with a hood and face mask covering everything but the eyes. However, the first mention of this black uniform does not occur until the year 1801. Since ninjas were frequently in disguise, pretending to be someone else, it's likely that most ninjas rarely wore the black uniform at all.

If a ninja snuck into a castle at night, the black uniform would be very useful. However, we know that the early uniforms were not completely black. They sometimes wore red uniforms. Ninjas liked to pretend they were invincible,

and if they got in a fight, the red in the uniform would hide bloodstains. No one would know they were hurt.

Sometimes ninjas wore lightweight armor under their uniforms. The ninjas liked people to believe they were invulnerable, and this hidden armor reinforced that idea.

Ninja sword

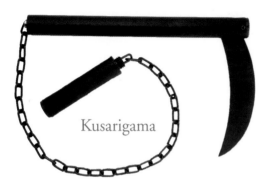

Kusarigama

Shuriken

The basic weapon of the ninja was the sword. It was shorter and straighter than the samurai sword, which made it better for straight-on thrust attacks.

One of the favorite weapons of the ninja was a *kusarigama.* It was a blade with a short handle and a weighted chain attached. The chain could block an opponent's sword. It could also catch an opponent, and then the blade could finish him off. The ninjas, always looking for a diversion, liked to set the weighted end of the chain on fire. If they were fighting at night, an opponent's eyes would focus on the flaming chain, and they would lose sight of the blade.

One favorite ninja weapon was the throwing star, or *shuriken*. It was a metal star-shaped object, with razor-sharp points. Contrary to how they are shown in movies, the throwing stars were not very accurate. They rarely, if ever, killed anyone. However, the thought of being struck by a shuriken in the forehead might keep someone from following a ninja, so they were useful tools.

Another ninja weapon was a *caltrop*. These were tiny nails welded together. When dropped, the caltrop came to rest on three prongs, with one prong sticking straight up. An unlucky person chasing a ninja could get a nail piercing up through his sandal into his foot. Again, this weapon did not kill, but it slowed down pursuers.

Caltrop

Sometimes ninjas used chemicals that acted like pepper spray. They could fling it in people's eyes, causing pain and giving the ninja time to escape. Some ninjas knew how to make chemicals that caused a small explosion, like a firecracker. This would startle everyone long enough for the ninjas to accomplish their mission. In fact, police today use a similar device called a flashbang. Police throw this type of grenade into a room, where it makes a loud noise and bright light. Criminals inside are confused and startled, giving police time to enter and arrest them.

When firearms made their way to Japan, the ninjas trained themselves how to use them. However, early firearms were not very accurate, and took a long time to reload. For a long time after firearms arrived, the bow and arrow was still a more effective long-distance weapon.

Ninjas used metal claw-like devices for climbing. They strapped the claws to their hands. The walls of most Japanese castles were rough and uneven. Using these claws, it was possible for ninjas to climb up the side of the castles.

Ninjas also had a variety of tools for breaking and entering. They had many tools to pick locks, or pry open wallboards.

NINJA MYTHS

Ninjas were surrounded in mystery and secrecy. Many myths emerged about what they could do. People were afraid of ninjas, so they often made up stories about their superhuman abilities. The ninjas themselves started many of these myths, so that people would fear them even more. Many of these myths are still with us today.

For example, a myth emerged that ninjas could disappear in a puff of smoke. Of course, they couldn't really disappear. However, ninjas knew how to use flash powder, which caused a bright light and smoke. While opponents shielded their eyes, the ninjas could burrow under a pile of leaves or climb a tree, or simply run away. When the opponent's eyes adjusted again, it looked like the ninja had disappeared into thin air.

Another myth that developed was that ninjas were not people at all, but ghosts. One ninja faked his own death so that when he came back, everyone thought he was a ghost. This struck terror into the hearts of his enemies.

Below: A "flying" ninja.

Some people said that ninjas could fly. Imagine people inside a city wall, watching a ninja effortlessly fly up from the other side and land on the top of the wall. They might spread the word that "ninjas can fly."

What the townspeople didn't see were the five other ninjas on the ground who formed a human pyramid, allowing the "flying" ninja to make a small leap to the top of the wall.

Above: Secrecy and stealth have fueled many myths about ninjas.

Above: Three lone ninjas on a hilltop.

Another myth emerged that ninjas could multiply themselves, or be in several places at once. This is probably due to the fact that several ninjas would invade a castle at the same time. Since they would wear the same uniform, they could easily be mistaken for the same person.

Some myths are still with us today. Many inaccuracies have been written about ninjas, and many of them perpetuate myths. One myth says ninjas can dislocate their own joints so they can escape from any restraint. This is ridiculous! Some books about ninjas reprint pictures of the famous "Trojan Cow Flamethrower." In this drawing, a ninja sits inside a fake cow and shoots flaming chemicals out of its mouth. No doubt, this drawing started as a joke, and someone believed it was real.

Sometimes people tried to explain a myth, and in doing so created another myth. For example, in medieval times people said ninjas could walk on water. In explaining this myth, modern ninja enthusiasts started another myth. They said ninjas strapped a device to their feet called a "water spider." The water spider was made of several pieces of lightweight wood that the ninjas wore on their feet, which allowed them to travel across the water.

While the water spider is certainly a creative idea, in reality it simply couldn't enable someone to walk on top of water. However, it's possible that if they sat on the device it might aid in buoyancy, like a life preserver.

Another fanciful explanation of the ninja's ability to walk on water is the use of buckets called *ukidaru*. By putting a foot in each bucket, and then using an oar, some people have said ninjas could float atop the water. Again, this device would be far too unstable to work. It's possible ninjas used the ukidaru when they were crossing water that was only a couple inches deep. That way, they could stay dry and not leave a trail of water as they snuck through an enemy encampment.

Below: Although some ninjas may have used buckets, called ukidaru, to walk on water, a more common method of crossing a castle moat was to use a rope with a hook attached, as seen in this 1801 illustration.

ARE THERE NINJAS TODAY?

The ninjas of medieval Japan no longer exist today. However, there are still people who do similar things. For example, in the United States there is a government agency called the Central Intelligence Agency (CIA). It gathers information on foreign groups that seek to harm people in the United States. Are there spies today? Are there secret agents today? Of course! Do they wear black uniforms and carry swords? No.

Below: Masaaki Hatsumi training one of his students in the art of ninjitsu.

However, the art of ninjitsu is still around today. It is difficult to say how different it is from the martial art used by medieval Japanese ninjas.

Masaaki Hatsumi is reported to be the 34th grandmaster of ninjitsu. This means that a master ninja handed down the techniques and tactics to one student, who then became the new grandmaster. When that grandmaster was old, he identified a new grandmaster from one of his students. That process happened 34 times, which led to the skills being passed on to Masaaki Hatsumi.

Masaaki Hatsumi teaches *taijitsu*, which is the unarmed fighting style of the ninjas. There is little need today to teach the other arts of the ninjas, except for historical study. However, today there are many ninjitsu schools, each claiming to know something about the ancient fighting art. Many of the instructors at these shady schools have had no training with Masaaki Hatsumi or his students.

Masaaki Hatsumi is widely respected as the most knowledgeable person about the ninja fighting arts. His first American student was Stephen Hayes, who now teaches in the United States.

Above: Masaaki Hatsumi works with students at his training gym in the town of Noda, Japan.

GLOSSARY

Clan

A group that is united because its members have something in common, like family, or geographic location. In medieval Japan, there was no single government until the beginning of the 1600s. Until that time, Japan was a collection of many warring clans, each with its own citizens and armies.

Joint lock

A submission technique, often used in jiu-jitsu, judo, and aikido, in which an attacker's arm or leg is twisted and held tight so that a joint, such as an elbow, knee, or ankle, is painfully overextended.

Medieval

In European history, a period defined by historians as roughly between 476 A.D. and 1450 A.D. In Japanese history, the medieval period, lasted longer than in Europe, extending into the 1800s before Japan began a rapid modernization of its society.

Mercenary

A person who is a professional soldier with no loyalty to a particular country or group, often someone hired to serve in a foreign army. Ninjas were mercenaries. They usually worked for whatever army would hire them.

Samurai

The trained warrior class of medieval Japan.

Seppuku

Ritual suicide performed by samurai when they were disgraced, especially after losing a battle. Also called *hara-kiri*.

Shogun

The military commander-in-chief of medieval Japan. In reality, most shoguns were forced to share power because of constantly shifting alliances between forces of the Japanese emperor and numerous warring clans.

Tactics

A plan or action used to achieve a specific goal. In warfare, tactics are a set of actions and maneuvers used to fight a battle or skirmish. Ninjas were employed and used as a tactic to disrupt the enemy. Strategy, on the other hand, is the overall planning of an entire war. Both are important, and closely related.
Sun Tzu, the famous general and philosopher of sixth-century B.C. China, wrote about tactics and strategy in his book *The Art of War*: "Strategy without tactics is the slowest route to victory. Tactics without strategy is the noise before defeat."

Warlord

A ruler or military commander of a town or region. Medieval Japan was often torn by conflicts among the many warlords ruling the countryside.

Samurai sword

INDEX

A

Asia 6

C

caltrop 23
Central
   Intelligence
   Agency (CIA)
   28

G

Gemban (general)
   12, 13

H

Hayes, Stephen
   29
Honshu 12

I

Iga 12

J

Japan 4, 5, 6, 11,
   12, 14, 23, 28

K

Koga 12
kusarigama 22

M

Masaaki Hatsumi
   28, 29

N

Nakagawa
   Shoshunjin 12,
   13
nightingale floor
   17

P

Pacific Ocean 6

S

samurai 4, 7, 8,
   11, 12, 18
seppuku 8
shinobi 4
shinobi-iri 19
shuriken 22

T

tai jutsu 18
taijitsu 29
Togakure Ryu 18
Tokugawa Ieyasu
   11
Trojan cow
   flamethrower
   26

U

Uesugi Kenshin
   17
ukidaru 27
United States 28,
   29

W

water spider 26,
   27